THE BUDDHA'S LAW AMONG THE BIRDS

THE BUDDHA'S LAW AMONG THE BIRDS

Translation & Commentary by
EDWARD CONZE

With a Preface by
J. BACOT

MOTILAL BANARSIDASS PUBLISHERS
PRIVATE LIMITED • DELHI

First Edition: Oxford, 1955
Reprint: Delhi, 1974, 1975, 1986, 1996

ISBN: 81-208-0198-9

Title of the Tibetan Original
Bya chos rin-cheṅ, phreṅ-ba

By arrangement with M/s Bruno Cassirer (Publishers) Ltd.

Also available at:

MOTILAL BANARSIDASS
41 U.A. Bungalow Road, Jawahar Nagar, Delhi 110 007
8, Mahalaxmi Chamber, Warden Road, Mumbai 400 026
120 Royapettah High Road, Mylapore, Madras 600 004
Sanas Plaza, Subhash Nagar, Pune 411 002
16 St. Mark's Road, Bangalore 560 001
8 Camac Street, Calcutta 700 017
Ashok Rajpath, Patna 800 004
Chowk, Varanasi 221 001

PRINTED IN INDIA

BY JAINENDRA PRAKASH JAIN AT SHRI JAINENDRA PRESS,
A-45 NARAINA, PHASE I, NEW DELHI 110 028
AND PUBLISHED BY NARENDRA PRAKASH JAIN FOR
MOTILAL BANARSIDASS PUBLISHERS PRIVATE LIMITED,
BUNGALOW ROAD, DELHI 110 007

The Buddha's Law among the Birds.

Turtle Dove

Crane

CONTENTS

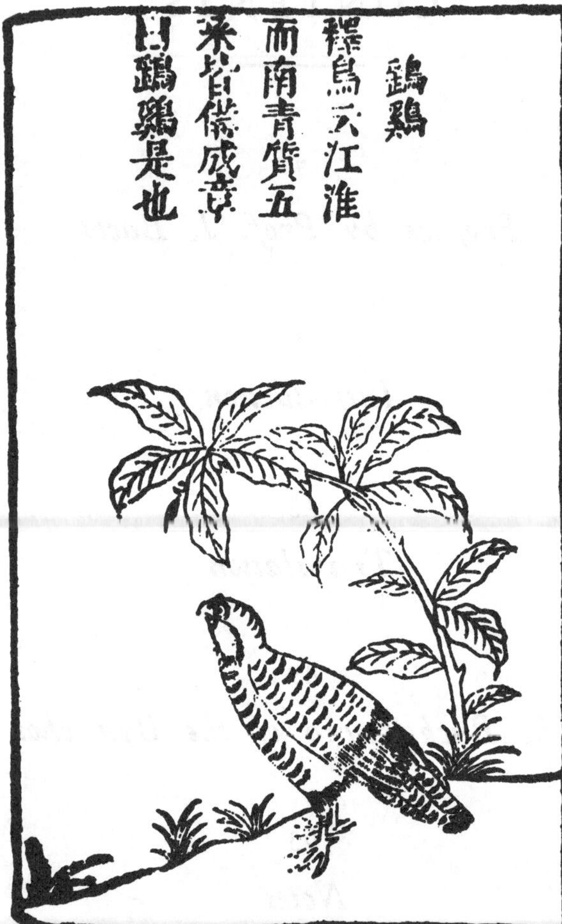

Kite

PREFACE

THE Western reader of this book, even if well versed in the literature of Buddhism, may still find it somewhat difficult to overcome his preconceived ideas regarding the animal world. In Europe a wide gulf separates man from even the most advanced species of animals, and a poem about Buddhism among birds may well strike him as nothing more than a literary fantasy. In India, however, this gulf was never more than a very shallow depression which could apparently be crossed with little effort. Even to-day, in India, one can see animals, both domesticated and wild, living together with mankind in conditions of familiarity which the Westerner finds unusual and at times even touching. The Buddhist concept of universality is not confined to man alone. It is a total universality which extends to all living creatures both above and below him, and it is this totality which is of the very essence of the doctrine. Thus a Council of Birds would neither offend nor seem strange to orthodox believers. The text here presented is a pious work of the same kind as the variations on the themes of the Jatakas, in which the literature of Tibet has found the majority of its edifying topics.

It is to a human being that merit is due for the conversion of the birds. According to a famous Tibetan novel their spokesman was an unfortunate Indian prince, an Avatar of Avalokita, and the son of a king of Benares, who by accident became a cuckoo. His story is one of the most charming that has ever come out of the inexhaustible fund of Indian legends.

Appearances may well belie the difficulty of the translator's task. In rendering the language which Tibetan Buddhists have put into the mouths of Himalayan birds whose habits, temperaments and sometimes even names are unknown to our ornithologists, he has faced greater problems than the arguments of more classical and more profound treatises would have presented. In consequence, if one encounters here and there an obscurity, we may perhaps attribute them in part to the mysteries inherent in the language of birds!

In Tibet, where printing is still comparatively little used, popular works are generally transmitted orally rather than by written record. Consequently they have remained little known to Western scholars. The rarity of copies of the *Precious Garland*, together with the originality of the subject, more than justify its publication. Here is an ingenious but eloquent testimony of the way in which the birds of the air came to share the disenchantment of mankind.

J. Bacot.

INTRODUCTION

THE Tibetan text of this charming book was first published in Calcutta in 1904, a slim volume of 40 pages. Satis Chandra Vidyabhushana, the editor, does not tell us whether his text was based on oral recitation, a manuscript or a blockprint. My translation, although made directly from the Tibetan, owes a great deal to the French translation by Henriette Meyer, brought out in 1953 by the Cahiers du Sud, under the title *Précieuse guirlande de la loi des oiseaux*. In the present state of Tibetan studies it is, however, not surprising that my French colleague and I should differ on many points of detail.

The work is anonymous and undated. The particularities of the language seem to point to the 17th or 18th century. The birds are content with a simple exposition of the beliefs and attitudes common to all Buddhists, and they do not take sides in the disputes of the sects. The theme of the book has, however, marked affinities to some of the tenets of the Kahgyudpa, *Bka'-brgyud-pa*, sect, and the author may well have been some Kahgyudpa lama who was content to remain anonymous. The Tibetan title, *Bya chos rin-chen 'phreṅ-ba*, means literally, "The Dharma among the Birds, a precious garland".

Both language and ideas mark this as a popular book, a piece of folk literature, destined for peasants and nomadic herdsmen. More than many a learned treatise, it conveys to us the emotional overtones of the religion which has ruled Tibet for so long, and it gives us some idea of what it feels like to be a Buddhist. The style is simple, straightforward and unsophisticated. Only the barest minimum of Buddhist technical terms is used, and they should offer little difficulty to the reader.

The *Dharma* is here, without any scholastic complications, just the doctrine of the Buddha. The *Three Treasures* are the Buddha, the Dharma, and the Order of monks, i.e. the three basic objects of Buddhist faith and devotion. *The samsaric world* is a term for this universe of transient phenomena in which we wander about so senselessly, and it is the opposite to Nirvana, the true goal of our lives. *State of Woe* is a technical term for rebirth as an animal, in hell, or as a ghost. The sanskrit is *durgati.* Although they are never far from a Buddhist's mind, the *States of Woe* are mentioned here with great frequency for the simple reason that the persons of the play are in one of them. *Muni* and *Jina* are two common epithets of the Buddha. The first means *Sage*, and the second *Victor*, or *Conqueror*. *Mara* is the personification of the principle of evil, the Buddhist devil or Satan. *Jambudvipa* in this context just means *India*. Sometimes I have retained the more accurate rendering of *wholesome* for *bde-ba* (*kuśala*), more often loosely translated as *good.* An act is *wholesome* if it brings merit, i.e. if it leads to greater happiness, either material or spiritual, in the future.

Although the translation aims at being faithful, I have tried, without adhering pedantically to the letter, to reproduce the spirit of the original and to convey the outlook on life of a people who have for centuries lived under the influence of Buddhist teachings. It will be interesting to see how Europeans will react to its message.

In the preparation of this work I owe a great deal to others. First of all I wish to express my gratitude to Professor J. Bacot, who has allowed us to reproduce here the Preface he wrote for the French translation. Mr. Peter Swann, of the Museum of Eastern Art in Oxford, has spared no pains to improve the diction of the translation. His name ought really to have appeared on the title page, together with mine. This would have been only just, – but justice is rarely done in this world. Further, I must thank my friend, Dr. Erik Haarh, of the Royal Library of Copenhagen, for so readily sending me photos from the work on pharmacy, which seems not to be found anywhere else in Europe. In addition the Ven. Tri-Khong, Dr. Haarh, Dr. Eichhorn and Dr. Newesky de Woikowicz have made valuable suggestions regarding both text and illustrations. The Librarian of the London School of Oriental and African Studies has very kindly given us access to their copy of the extremely rare Ming encyclopedia. Part of the translation has previously appeared in the *Middle Way*, and I want to thank the editor for her permission to reprint it here.

London *Edward Conze*
January 1955

Young Crow

The Lord Buddha has said:

IN THE LANGUAGE OF ANGELS,
OF SERPENTS, OF FAIRIES,
IN THE SPEECH OF THE DEMONS,
THE TALK OF THE HUMANS,
IN THEM ALL I'VE EXPOUNDED
THE DHARMA'S DEEP TEACHINGS,
AND
IN ANY TONGUE
THAT A BEING MAY GRASP THEM.

Sparrow Hawk

ONCE UPON A TIME,

in the course of this our auspicious aeon,[1] there was to be found, on the border between India and Tibet, a beautiful wooded mountain. «Pleasant Jewel» was its name, and it was a holy retreat for Saraha, the great magician,[2] and many other saints who dwelt in seclusion among the summits of the Himalayas, which shine in all the splendour of perfect whiteness. Here are found glaciers, like lions with manes of turquoise displaying their majesty. All along the slopes of the mountain, far to the East and South, live countless birds of good omen, birds like the white grouse, and others, and also a great many animals, – stags, argalis, antelopes and others, all happily playing and frolicking free from care.

The South, West and North are adorned with many and varied trees, with forests of sandalwood, aloewood, myrobalan, olive, walnut and birch. Magnificent rocks give to the four sides of the mountain an aspect of supreme beauty. All around the foot of that mountain, live royal birds, like King Vultures, eagles and others, giving themselves up to the pleasures of flight. There are lakes, ponds, pools, water-meadows, and stretches of water which have

[1] *For Notes see p. 63*

flown down from the cliffs, rocks and glaciers. These gurgling, murmuring waters are graced with many kinds of water birds, with geese, swamp birds and black terns. Tree-birds adorn the forest heights, – peacocks, parrots skilled in the art of speech, thrushes, crows, and others. This is the precious mountain with its forests.

Owl (?)

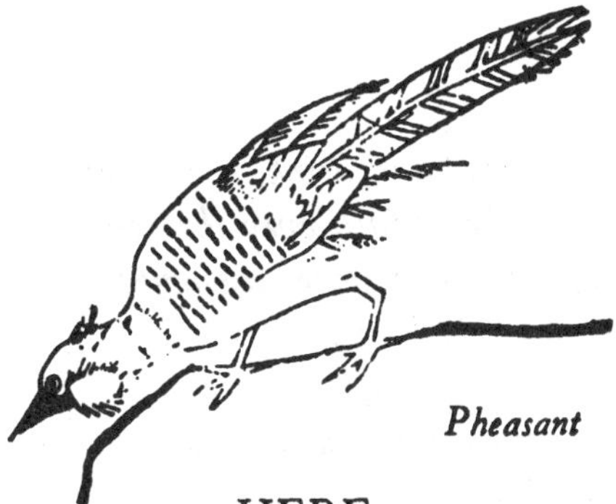

Pheasant

HERE,

IN ORDER TO TEACH THE DHARMA

unto the feathered folk, the holy Lord Avalokita, who had transformed himself into a Cuckoo, the great king of the birds, sat for many years day and night under a large sandalwood tree, immobile and in perfect trance.

One day Master Parrot came before the Great Bird, and addressed him, saying:

«Greetings O great and noble bird!
For one whole year, until to-day,
You've sat there crouching, motionless,
In the cool shade of a Santal tree.
So silent, dumb and speechless;
Does something anger or disturb your heart?
When, O Great Bird, your trance has ended,
Will you accept these seeds, the fine quintessence of all food?»

And thus replied the Great Bird:

«Listen then, O parrot skilled in speech!
I have surveyed[3] *this ocean of Samsara,*
And I have found nothing substantial in it.
Down to the very last, I saw the generations die,

They killed for food and drink, – how pitiful!
I saw the strongholds fall, even the newest,
The work of earth and stones consumed, – how pitiful!
Foes will remove the hoarded spoils
down to the very last,
Oh to have avidly gathered this wealth, and hidden it,
– how pitiful!
Closest friends will be parted, down to the very last,
Oh, to have formed those loving thoughts of affection,
– how pitiful!
Sons will side with the enemy, – even to the youngest,
Oh to have given that care to those who were born of
one's body, – how pitiful!
Relatives united and intimate friends,
Children reared, and riches stored,
All are impermanent, like an illusion,
And nothing substantial is found in them.
My mind has now forsaken all activity.
So that I may keep constant to my vows,
Here, in the cool shade of a Santal tree
I dwell in solitude and silence,
In trance I meditate, from all distractions far removed.
Go thou, – repeat this speech of mine
To all large birds, and to all feathered creatures! »

The Parrot, skilled in speech, then gave a signal to all the birds, both large and small, who thereupon arrived from all sides, – the Indian birds led by the Peacock, the Tibetan birds by the Vulture, the water birds led by the Goose, the tree-birds by the Parrot, the birds of good omen by the White Grouse, and the domestic birds by the red-breasted Cock. And so it was until all the birds had assembled. They then came before the Great Bird with a request to be taught the Dharma. And the peacock, as leader of all the birds from India, arranged his followers in rows on the right, while the vulture, as head of the Tibetan birds, arranged his in rows on the left.

The Parrot, skilled in speech, then rose from the middle of the ranks, and, swaying like a bamboo hurdle, saluted three times and spoke as follows:

«Greetings, you great and noble bird!
Though you are weary and disgusted with Samsara,
We beg you, give a little thought to us!
Ignorant and deluded creatures that we are;
The effects of many misdeeds in our past
Have tied us to this suffering, bound us, chained us.
We beg of you the good Dharma freeing us
from suffering,
We beg the light dispelling all our ignorance,
We beg from you the Dharma,
– the cure of all defilements,
Birds of every kind assembled here,
We beg of you the good Dharma,
that we may ponder on it.»

Thrice the Great Bird shook his wings, and then he said: *«Cuckoo!»*

«You birds assembled here, without distraction listen
– Koo!

To these three exhortations I deliver here: – Koo!
Reflect in earnest on impermanence and on death, – Koo!
Commit in no way any evil deed, – Koo!
Release within yourselves
the good and wholesome thoughts! – Koo!
In this and in the after life
the Three Treasures are a safe refuge, – Koo!
Venerating them brings blessings from on high, – Koo!
Keep regular in your petitions to them! – Koo!
These are my wishes for your happiness in this life: – Koo!
Abandon all attachments, wherever they may be, – Koo!
Be diligent in performance of your tasks, – Koo!
Then you will gain a lasting happiness. – Koo!
The objects of activities are altogether vain, – Koo!
Put your inmost minds into a state of non-action, – Koo!
For this is the thought of the Jina himself. – Koo!
For seven days meditate on these precepts, – Koo!
And then return to me, – Koo!

All the birds thereupon meditated on this discourse which had so pleased their ears for seven days without allowing themselves to be distracted in any way. On the morning after these seven days had elapsed, the Great Bird spoke again as follows:

«Smoke a sign of fire is,
The Southern cloud a sign of rain.
The little child will be a man,
The foal a stallion one day.

Deep thinking about death will lead to the unique and worthy Dharma. The rejection of attachment to the wheel of Samsara, the belief in the retribution of all deeds, mindfulness of the impermanence and mortality of this life, – these are signs that we approach the unique, worthy Dharma. O Birds assembled here, is there anything of this nature in your minds? Tell me then your thoughts!»

Thereupon the King Vulture rose from the ranks on the left, shook his wings three times, and said:

«One must open one's ears to such beneficial discourse.
One must know the folly of this ceaseless busyness.
One must know the True Dharma to be the basis
of freedom.[4]
One must know that born, one cannot stay,
that one must die.
One must know that hoarded wealth must be dissipated.
One must know that gifts now given are provisions
for the future.
One must know that a state of woe is the fruit
of evil deeds.
One must know that all happiness is the fruit of
good deeds.
Through lasting merit alone can happiness be achieved.»

Then the Great Crane rose, stretched his neck three times, and said: *sruṅ dgos*, which means, *one must observe.*

«One must observe unsullied moral purity
as the root of all dharmic action.
One must observe the need to abandon
whatever belongs to this world, and that includes
the bonds of life in the various heavens.

One must observe that indolence and sloth hinder
the doing of good.
One must observe that the demons of meanness
hinders generosity.
Let these things also enter well into your minds.»

Thereupon the Golden Goose rose, shook his wings three times, and said: *ṅaṅ stud ṅaṅ stud*, which means, *that prolongs the bondage, that prolongs the bondage.*

«To remain from birth to death without the Good Law,
– that prolongs the bondage.
To desire emancipation, and still deserve a state of
woe, – that prolongs the bondage.
To hope for miraculous blessings, and still have
wrong opinions, – that prolongs the bondage.
To neglect those things which turn the mind
towards salvation, – that prolongs the bondage.
To strive for purity of vision, and yet be blinded
by a faulty judgment, – that prolongs the bondage.
To give and yet be checked by meanness,
– that prolongs the bondage.
To aim at lasting achievements while still exposed
to this world's distractions, – that prolongs the bondage.
To try to understand one's inner mind
while still chained to hopes and fears,
– that prolongs the bondage.
All you who thus prolong your bondage
within this ocean of suffering,
Try to grasp the meaning of my words,
for they will shorten your bondage.»

Thereupon the Raven with his great wings rose, made a few sideways steps, and said: *grogs yoṅ grogs yoṅ*, which means, *help will come, help will come.*

«When you have been true to your vows, help will come in the form of a happy life among men.
When you have given gifts, help will come in the form of future wealth.
When you have performed the acts of worship, help will come from the guardian angels.
When your solemn promises are made in all good faith, help will come from the love of the fairies.[6]
When you are alert at the sacrificial festivals, help will come from the Guardians of the Dharma.
When in this life you learn to enter into higher meditation, help will come from the future Buddha.[7]
Learn therefore to gain these virtues, for help comes through them.»

Thereupon the little Wagtail rose, sharpened his beak three times, and said: *gtiṅ riṅ*, which means, *deep and vast.*

«Deep and vast, this ocean of ills, this world of Samsara.
Deep and vast, these hells for the evil-doer.
Deep and vast, this gulf of the states of woe.
Deep and vast, the promptings of worldly thought.
Deep and vast, the cravings for food and dress.
Deep and vast, the fetters of love of self.
Deep and vast, the aftermath of evil habits.
Deep and vast, the morass of wicked deeds.
Let us, then, make ready to leave this world of Samsara, which is so deep and vast.»

Thereupon the great Ruddy Sheldrake rose and said: *os gtor os gtor*, which means, *one must do without, one must do without.*

«Dwelling in the world of Samsara one must do without bliss.
Without the celestial Dharma, one must do without deliverance.
Without reward earned for past gifts, one must do without all riches.
Without devotion, one must do without the blessings from on high.
When personal worth is small, one must do without a spiritual guide.
Without wisdom, one must do without virtues.
When leading a homeless life, one must do without affection.
Without a good character one must do without companions.
When one commits offences with women one must do without capacity for deeds of lasting worth.»

Thereupon the heavenly White Grouse rose, flapped his wings three times, and said:

«Hard to fathom the full extent of ills in this round of Samsara.
Hard to fathom the totality of causes and effects.
Hard to fathom the limit of endless mundane actions.
Hard to fathom this body, which entails so much delusion and such tumult.
Hard to fathom the deceits of parents.

Hard to fathom the religious ways of frauds.
Hard to fathom the religious talk of the shallow.
Hard to fathom the mischievous unrest aroused by chiefs.
Hard to fathom the virtues of the skilful.
Hard to fathom the choice of action:
For in the end all comes to naught.»

Thereupon the Pigeon rose, circled three times in the air, and said: *yi mug*, *yi mug*, which means, *well might one despair, well might one despair.*

«Well might one despair, – the degenerate men
of this iron age![8]
Well might one despair, – the conduct of evil men!
Well might one despair, – the quarrels
of families in disunion!
Well might one despair, – the absurdities
of jealous neighbours!
Well might one despair – the mischievous disputes
of great and passionate men!
Well might one despair, – the poison running through
the deeds of mischief makers!
Well might one despair, – the pursuits of the busybodies!
Well might one despair, – the chatterings of the garrulous!
Well might one despair, – the enemies of the Dharma
who teach it wrongly!
Well might one despair, – the squanderings
of ill-gained food and wealth!
Well might one despair, – the swindlers
who adulterate our food!
Well might one despair, – those who would here abide
for ever, however certain of impermanence and death!

Well might one despair, – the children raised with tenderness who then reject their parents!
Well might one despair, – the intimate friends unconfident in separation!
Well might one despair, – the cares of family life we leave with such regret!
Well might one despair, – false friends returning evil for our kindness!
Because they cause despair, shun all such things!»

Thereupon the Dove rose, and said: *skyid dgug-pas sdug thug*, which means, *the quest for bliss will lead to ill.*

«The quest for bliss in this samsaric world will lead to ills in a state of woe.
The quest for bliss in earthly things will lead to ills which never end.
The quest for bliss in family life will lead to untold ills.
The quest for bliss through avarice will lead to ills of hunger and thirst.[9]
The quest for bliss through gay diversions will lead to ills of restlessness.
The quest for bliss in common things will lead to ills of body and of mind.
The quest for bliss in earthly joys will lead to the ills of effort.
Such are the things which lead to ill. Indeed so it is!»

Thereupon the Jackdaw rose, bent his head three times, and said: *khu skyuṅ khu skyuṅ*, which means, *Khu, leave behind! Khu, leave behind!*

«Leave behind this world of endless activity!
Leave behind that desire to act which brings
unending weariness!
Leave behind that pious talk which leaves your own
nature unchecked!
Leave behind those brave sayings wherein fine words
conceal an evil heart!
Leave behind that urge for finery which is not yours!
Leave behind that urge towards success yet knowing not
how to pray!
Leave behind that urge for greatness when you cannot
bear its burden!
Leave behind those admonitions when you have not
learnt to listen!
Leave behind those angry brawls unworthy even
of wild bears!
Leave behind those religious acts which are
mere hypocrisy!
In short, how plentiful indeed this world's activities
which one should leave behind!»

Thereupon the Owl rose, ruffled her feathers, and said: *'u sdug 'u sdug*, which means, *what misery! what misery!*

«The hour of death without insight from meditation,
– what misery!
A priest without morals, – what misery!
An old lama without judgment, – what misery!
A chieftain without authority, – what misery!
A general without troops, – what misery!
A king without counsellors, – what misery!

A leader without followers, – what misery!
A teacher without virtues, – what misery!
A disciple without deference, – what misery!
A friend not to be trusted, – what misery!
A household without a common purpose, – what misery!
Knowing the misery that all these things can bring,
– avoid them!»

Thereupon the Cock, the domestic bird, rose, flapped his wings three times, and said: *e go e go*, which means, *do you understand that? Do you understand that?*

«Whilst you live in this samsaric world, no lasting
happiness can be yours, – do you understand that?
To the performance of worldly actions there is no end,
– do you understand that?
In flesh and blood there is no permanence,
– do you understand that?
The presence, at all times, of Mara, the Lord of Death,
– do you understand that?
Even the rich man, when he is laid low, departs alone,
– do you understand that?
He has no strength to take the wealth he gathered,
– do you understand that?
Our bodies, so dear to us, will feed the birds and dogs,
– do you understand that?
Wherever the mind may go, it cannot control its fate,
– do you understand that?
We are bound to lose those we love and trust,
– do you understand that?

Punishment follows the evil we do,
– do you understand that?
Wherever one looks, nothing is there substantial,
– do you understand that?»

The Lark, weary at heart from her countless rebirths, then wept and said: *skyid skyur skyid skyur*, which means, *the pleasures turn sour, the pleasures turn sour.*

«When they dwell in a state of woe, the pleasures
of beings turn sour.
After the births and deaths of the past, the pleasures
expected from future rebirth turn sour.
Seeing others enjoy one's gains, the pleasures of storing up
wealth turn sour.
Seeing the crops destroyed by weeds and hail,
the pleasures of tilling the earth turn sour.
Seeing aged parents turned from house and home,
the pleasures of raising children turn sour.
Since, when the time has come, one must depart without it,
the pleasures of love for the body turn sour.
Since, when the time comes, one must depart alone,
the pleasures of love of friends turn sour.
Seeing the corpses laid in the burial ground, the pleasures
of pride in this bodily citadel turn sour.»

And she continued:

«Since these pleasures all turn sour, what use are all
these things?
What use this homely existence, – a source of suffering?
What use these families rent by strife, yet even in
unhappiness not parting?

What use are sons, when their upbringing is so profitless?
What use are friends when they are not sincere in our defence?
What use possessions when one knows not how to use them?
What use these fortresses, – without defence against the Lord of Death?
What use these chieftains who spread misery and death?
What use in this unrighteous world to eat and thus maintain the body?[10]
What use religious talk to those who have learnt little and can understand still less ?
What use concern for others' good when one is full of selfish interest?
What use these moral rules with no attempt to follow them?
What use, therefore, these many things, – useless indeed are they!»

Thereupon the little red Lagopus rose, looked from the corner of his eye, and said: *tig tig med*, which means, *no certainty.*

«*For an imperfect yogin, – no certainty!*[11]
In a dharma which transcends the whole of Samsara, – no certainty![12]
In a rumour which has travelled far, – no certainty!
In the talk of a seasoned liar, – no certainty!
In the gossip of the garrulous, – no certainty!
In the affairs of busybodies, – no certainty!
In the conversation of the stupid, – no certainty!
In possessions near to enemy lands, – no certainty!

In the moment of death, once one is born, – no certainty!
In the speech of the ever deceitful, – no certainty!
In the yield of the barley crop, – no certainty!
In the mind of a fool, – no certainty!
In a woman's control of the household, – no certainty!
In the wanderings of a stray dog, – no certainty!
In the rain from a summer sky, – no certainty![13]
For the husband of the whore, – no certainty!
In the walk of the bow-legged, – no certainty!
In the friendship of beings, – no certainty!»

The red-beaked Chinese Thrush then rose, and said: *bcud loṅ bcud loṅ*, which means, *profit from*, *profit from*.

«*Profit from the holy teachings once you have gained a human form!*
Profit from the holy Dharma, and achieve your aims!
Profit from your possessions, and give them all away!
Profit from the pure doctrine, and choose a lowly place!
Profit from your knowledge, and meditate upon the guardian gods!
Profit from your discontent, withdraw yourself from this samsaric world!
Profit from the Buddha, awake to the essence of absolute thought!»

Next the Peacock in all his splendour rose, displayed his tail three times, and said: *kog go kog go*, which means, *yours is the loss*, *yours is the loss*.

«*If you must dwell in a state of woe, yours is the loss of happiness.*

If you cannot have the Good Law, yours is the loss
of the Buddha.
If you have no will to give, yours is the loss of pleasure
in possessions.
If nothing vital is achieved, yours is the loss
of your labour.
In dealing with the treacherous, yours is the loss
of confidence.
In new friendships, yours is the loss of sureness
in their constancy.
As for the self-complacent, – theirs is the loss
of judgment;
As for the hate-ridden, – theirs is the loss of
higher opportunities;
As for the mean, – theirs is the loss of chance to offer gifts;
As for the stubborn, – theirs is the loss of self-possession;
As for the mistrustful, – theirs is the loss of logical abilities;
As for the defiled, – theirs is the loss of the Good Law;
As for the disbelievers, – theirs is the loss of all
miraculous blessings;
For no one can change the laws of this samsaric world.»

The Indian Kestrel then rose, and said: *Ki ki.*

«Observe this king who has lived too long. He is now no
more than a common man, Ki ki.
Observe this man not content with what he has. He will
surely be crushed by his foes, Ki ki.
Observe this man who ignores the fruits of his evil deeds.
He will surely go to hell, Ki ki.
Observe this man who calculates on staying here for ever.
He will surely be ensnared by death, Ki ki.

Observe these wild men, robbers and thieves. They will surely be punished by the judge, Ki ki.
Observe these unrighteous men of false views. They are a disgrace to the Three Treasures, Ki ki.
All those who see their evil thoughts and deeds accumulate before their eyes, – let them be mindful of the consequences, Ki ki!»

Then from the centre of the ranks rose the Parrot, skilled in speech, and said:

«Listen you beings of this samsaric world:
What you desire is happiness, what you find is grief.
While you inhabit a state of woe, salvation is not yet at hand.
Thinking on this must make me sad.
I now recall the good, the unique Law;
Hear it, you denizens of this samsaric world,
Perennial for time without beginning.
Because its benefits are so immense,
Let us here recall that unique Dharma:
‹These ills in our state of woe are but the fruits of evil deeds,
The karmic outcome of your own accumulated acts;
For you and only you could make them.›
So now strip off the veil that clouds your thoughts:
This life, like dew on grass, is but impermanent,
And your remaining here for ever out of question.
So here and now, think on these things, and make your effort!
‹The pain from heat and cold in hell,
The hunger and the thirst which Pretas[14] feel,

All are the fruits of evil deeds.› So has the Muni spoken.
Here, from within my heart, I make the vow
To shun all evil, to achieve the good.
From deep within my heart I seek my refuge
In the Three Treasures ever changeless,
Never failing, never fading,
Our precious ally through the whole of time.
In my mind, now free from doubt, is faith established.
Resolved to know the holy Dharma,
I now reject all things in this samsaric world.
And so, you great and noble bird,
We, this assembly, beg you grant us
Your esteemed instruction, teach us to understand the nature of all life!»

So he spoke, and made three salutations.

Thereupon the Cuckoo, the Great Bird, spoke as follows:

«Birds, large and small assembled here, well have you understood. In all the speeches you have made not one has denied the truth. Well have you spoken, well indeed! With undistracted mind keep well these words within your hearts. And so, O birds assembled here, the large birds and also the little youngsters lucky to be here, hear me with reverence and attention!
The things of this samsaric world are all illusion, like a dream.
Where'er one looks, where is their substance?
Palaces built of earth and stone and wood,
Wealthy men endowed with food and dress and finery,

Legions of retainers who throng round the mighty, –
These are like castles in the air, like rainbows in the sky.
And how deluded those who think of this as truth!
When uncles – nephews – brothers – sisters gather as kindred do,
When couples and children gather as families do,
When friends and neighbours gather in good fellowship, –
These are like meetings of dream friends, like travellers sharing food with strangers.
And how deluded those who think of this as truth!
This phantom body grown in uterine water from a union of seed and blood[15]*,–*
Our habitual passions springing from the bad deeds of our past,
Our thoughts provoked by divers apparitions, –
All are like flowers in autumn, clouds across the sky.
How deluded, O assembled birds, if you have thought of them as permanent.
The splendid plumage of the peacock with its many hues,
Our melodious words in which notes high and low are mingled,
The link of causes and effects which now have brought us here together, –
They are like the sound of echoes, the sport of a game of illusion.
Meditate on this illusion, do not seize on them as truth!
Mists on a lake, clouds across a southern sky,
Spray blown by wind above the sea,
Lush fruits ripened by the summer sun, –
In permanence they cannot last; in a trice they separate and fall away.

Meditate on their illusion, do not think of them as permanent!»

The Great Bird then continued:

«Certain indeed it therefore is that these our speeches, like our happiness in this samsaric world, the trivial joys of this our life on earth, are like a magical illusion, like a dream, a rainbow in the sky, the echo of a voice shouted into a deserted valley. These similes have all been taught (by the Lord Buddha) to show that these things have no permanence and no abiding substance.

Again, consider then the total lack of substance in this samsaric world! Hold fast to the Three Treasures, – safe refuge never failing! Clothe yourselves in the good Dharma, – the hope of this and the after life! Reduce your wants, – for death comes soon! Cut off from all attachments, – separation from your friends is certain! Hold not to anything as truth, – it is all illusion whatever it may be: All the elements of this samsaric world and of Nirvana, – all are the products of your own thought. Pure thought in its beginning is not distracted by any object whatsoever. It is empty and impersonal, unproduced, unstopped, it stays not, neither does it go nor come. If one seeks it, one finds it not; if one looks for it, one sees it not. There is nothing that has perfect and complete reality. It cannot withstand analysis, – for that splits its seeming unity into multiplicity. That is why it is not perfect and complete. Mark in your minds the true nature of all conditioned things. The fully enlightened Buddhas of the past have taught that these are non-existent, – not to be described in words. Meditate with undistracted minds their precepts which are the fruits of unconditioned knowledge. All those here assembled are assembled in a dream. All birth is but a dream-birth, all death a dream-death. Buddhas are only dream-Buddhas, and those who drift about caught in the cycle of birth-and-death do so only in a dream. How can one know oneself by oneself? Even though the root of error be cut off, still not a single atom of a perfect truth can be discovered. You must therefore seek salvation in your own Thought![16] *I have placed your task before you.*»

The Cuckoo, the Great Bird, continued:

«*Now all of you met here and now, – you all will gain in happiness if only you can act for others. Spread the good word of the Dharma, and the fruits of that act will bring you benefits.*

Next year, in the fifth Turkish month, we will meet again in Yalung, the great land of the birds, where in that fertile spot we shall be still more numerous. Then, O Birds of Tibet, shall we meet again. Till then may all of you enjoy good health! And henceforth may you never lose the spirit of the Dharma! And pass some of the Dharma's precepts to the small birds, even to the very tiny ones who could not join us here.»

Thereupon each bird in turn made an offering of food and fruits to the Great Bird, performed a salutation, and returned each one to his own home. Instantly the Great Bird entered into a perfect trance.

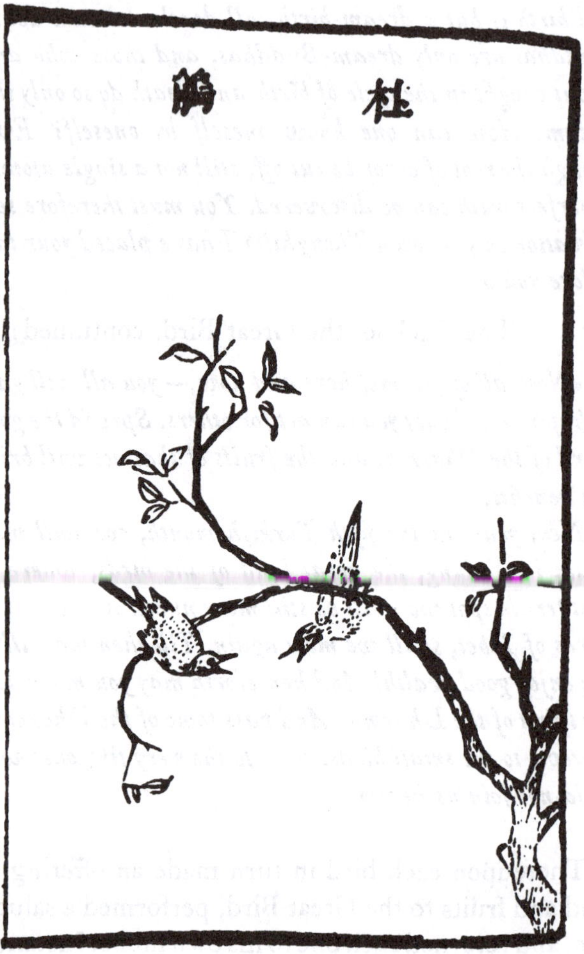

Cuckoos

THE FOLLOWING YEAR,

at the beginning of the fifth Turkish month, the Great Bird emerged from his trance, and went to Tibet. The birds, ever more numerous, flew rapidly over the woods of Yalung, the great land of the birds. All the Tibetan birds came to Yalung to wait upon the Great Bird and beg of him the Dharma. Like a swaying bamboo hurdle they appeared when first they greeted him. They felt great joy and ardour in their hearts. With the King Vulture and others at their head, they uttered with one voice the following request:

«Greetings, you great and noble bird.
In the year since last we met,
Has your body been in health,
Your mind turned deeper into trance?
Have you continued teaching Dharma
To birds in this samsaric world?
Were you wearied by your journey here?
Did you take care in coming to Tibet?
On all great birds assembled here,
Kindly bestow again your favour!
We beg again some Dharma which befits our minds.»

The Great Bird smiled, and spoke as follows:

«O birds, both large and small assembled here,
I wish you well.
In the year now past until to-day,
In body free from sickness, and with happy mind,
In the cool shade of a Santal tree,
I felt the ecstasy of trance increasing in my mind.
Having withdrawn from all distraction,
I felt the beatitude of well-achieved seclusion.
Having rejected greed and hate, those bad companions,
I felt the lonely ecstasy of transic meditation.
Intensively I turned the wheel of Dharma
For the birds of the land of India.
On my journey to Tibet
I had no cause for weariness of body or of mind.
Glad am I to reach Yalung, this country of the birds,
Great happiness I feel in this most fertile place.
O Birds of Tibet, assembled here, are you content
in body and in mind?
Auspicious the trend of events which allowed us
here to meet again alive!»

Thereupon the Guru of the small birds rose, made his three salutations, and said:

«Greetings, you great Cuckoo of wide renown!
Fair to see your body's beauty,
Sweet to hear your gentle words,
Meek and friendly is your nature,
Devoted from compassion to enlighten us.[17]
A learned Indian bird, coming to Tibet,

To this great flock of small and tiny birds,
Who did not meet before 'twixt India and Tibet,
Extend to us the kindness of your heart.
We beg such Dharma as befits the mind of each.»

The Great Bird then rejoiced and smiled, saying:

«*Cuckoo! So be it, little birds! Excellent is your request for the Dharma. Certainly it comes as a consequence of your bright deeds in earlier times.*»

He then went on to expound the Dharma in such a way that it could be understood by all birds, large and small, good and bad. His discourse was beneficial to their hearts, spreading a salutary understanding through their minds.

The ill-omened birds, who had kept their distance from the Great Bird, heard the reception given him. From among them the Owlet rose, made his three salutations, bowed low and said: *sbu khaṅ sbu khaṅ*, which means, *are their hearts at ease?*

«*Those beings who dwell in this samsaric world,*
– are their hearts at ease?
All beings with their sufferings, – are their hearts at ease?
Those suffering in hell, – are their hearts at ease?
The haughty with all their might, – are their
hearts at ease?
Bad men ruling the earth, – are their hearts at ease?
Cheats with all their money, – are their hearts at ease?
The eight worldly dharmas[18] *and a respectable*
appearance, – do they put the heart at ease?

The jealousies of bad neighbours, – do they
put the heart at ease?
The evil thoughts of unharmonious companions,
– do they put the heart at ease?
Mistaken views of bad pupils, – do they put the
heart at ease?
Each one seeks his own peace, – but rarely does he find it.»

Thereupon the Partridge rose, made his salutations, and said: *spros bral yin, spros bral yin*, which means, *it must fail you, it must fail you.*

«*When you dwell in this samsaric world,*
happiness must fail you.
When no longer you are active, wealth must fail you.
In bad company, your yearning for friendship
must fail you.
When you have evil thoughts, your salvation
must fail you.
With those possessed by hate, your compassion
must fail you.
Caught in the rush of life, your ability to meditate
must fail you.
With the impious, your faith must fail you.
If the supreme Dharma does not guide you,
everything you do must fail you.»

Then rose the Hoopoe who made his triple salutation and exclaimed, *mi 'ju kha tsha, mi 'ju kha tsha*, which means, *avoid it, for it burns the mouth; avoid it, for it burns the mouth.*[19]

«The wealth which swindlers amass through their deceit,
– avoid it, for it burns the mouth!
The wealth which robbers have snatched in raids, –
avoid it, for it burns the mouth!
Auspicious food refused to some great meditator by the
master of a house, – avoid it, for it burns the mouth!
The riches of the gullible fleeced by rogues,
– avoid them, for they burn the mouth!
The share of food withheld from the deceased at funeral
repasts,[20] *– avoid it, for it burns the mouth!*
All these world systems, – avoid them, for
they burn the mouth!
Under a glaring sun in a cloudless sky
Ephemeral aggregates,[21] *stuff of illusion,*
Fed on foods which burn the mouth!»

Then the Cuckoo, the Great Bird, rose again
and said:

«Now will I teach unto you a Dharma deep but comprehensible to each and every one. Listen with reverence and undistracted minds!»

Then he continued:

«Alas, the flowers last year so beautiful,
– next year to be destroyed by frost;
so, too, will disappear this transient interlude,
a mere illusion.
The rainbow, so beautiful in all its hues,
fades away to nothingness;
so, too, will disappear these festive robes,
for all their finery.

However clear the voice and strong its echo, it cannot last;
so, too, the mighty of this earth for all their greatness.
Those who visit fairs and markets soon disperse again;
so, too, our families, friends and companions,
for all their number.
Honey stored by bees for them alone can serve no other;
so, too, material wealth, for all its abundance.
The business of the world is but a game for children.
Though body and speech be smashed to dust,
their aftermath lives on.
Forsake this world, – for it is all imposture, all illusion.
Treasure, O all assembled birds, the Dharma all supreme,
the greatest benefactor!
In the end will the body lose its health;
Well is it ere this to have reached the true goal of living.
In the end will all accumulated wealth be consumed;
Well is it, while it lasted, to have given alms.
In the end will bonds of families and friends be cut;
Well is it now to break off all attachments.
In the end will fall this castle with its walls;
Well is it to remain content in solitary homelessness.
Reliance on a chieftain only ends in heavy labour;
Well is it then to follow some holy Lama.
In this world all achievements must end in ruin;
Well is it then to turn away from false desires.
The supreme Dharma, – that is the source of lasting merit
now and in the future;
It is well to teach it here below.
The Three Treasures, – these are the everlasting refuge,
now and in the future;
It is well to beseech them here below.

Afflicted by love, beings try to quench their thirst
From the waters of an alluring mirage.
How much better to meditate!
Renounce therefore this samsaric world, and treasure the supreme Dharma!»

The Great Bird then continued:

«Now that you have achieved a certain knowledge of the Dharma, and arrived at a belief in the law of karma, let each of you herewith make a promise!»

And he went on to say:

«Exert yourselves in the bright acts of merit, and shun the dark acts of evil! Let all now firmly promise some improvement!»

The King Vulture then promised not to kill another living being. *The White Grouse*, the heavenly bird, promised henceforth to live only in mountain ranges, never to descend into the valleys. *The Goose* promised to seek his food only from the waters and the swamps. *The Indian Kestrel* promised to spend but one hour a day on food. *The Pigeon* promised to make his home in the hollow of a rock-cavern, and to respect the Stupas and the shrines.[22] *The Lark*, one of the smaller birds, promised to offer worship to the Three Treasures with melodious song. *The Cock*, the domestic bird, promised no more to violate the dawn. *The Hoopoe* promised to make the caves his winter home.[23] And all the birds, both large and small, promised not to gather food above their daily needs.

Only *the Raven* and *the Kite*, from habitual avarice, would make no promises at all.

Then spoke the Great Bird once again:

«*Henceforth let this be your Dharma! O Tibetan birds, you who have prospered here in Tibet, join your songs in harmony with those of the other birds!*»

When he finished speaking, the birds all rose with joy, danced awhile through the air, and sang their songs.

Happiness be yours and gladness too, – may you prosper!» said the Great Bird, happy that he had come there. «*Cuckoo, cuckoo,*» he sang, «*the light shed by the Dharma of the Birds brings me happiness. In joy and gladness leap and sway together in this graceful dance! Sing your songs and may you thrive!*»

«*May you prosper, may you prosper,*» he said, happy to be in that plentiful land. «*Cuckoo, cuckoo,*» he sang, «*I am happy because the essence of the Dharma of the Birds has enriched you. In joy and gladness leap and sway together in this graceful dance! Sing your songs, and may you thrive!*»

«*Cu cu, ci ci,*» he said, glad that all these hosts of birds had come together. «*Cuckoo, cuckoo,*» he sang, «*I am happy because I could give you the Dharma of the Birds. In joy and gladness leap and sway together in this graceful dance! Sing your songs, and may you thrive! Sing your happy songs which carry far! Dance your greatly joyful dance! Now you have won your hearts' desire.*»

All the birds sang happy songs, leapt up and danced with gladness, and wished each other good fortune and abounding joy. They then accompanied the Great Bird for one whole day, and the Great Bird without mishap returned to India. On their way back, the birds of Tibet slept all together under a tree. The next day, when the sun of Jambudvipa rose, thrice they circled the tree where they had met, exchanged their hopes for another such joyful meeting, and each one, satisfied, returned on wings to his dwelling place.

Here ends
THE PRECIOUS GARLAND
OF THE DHARMA OF THE BIRDS.

Cock

Skyar-mo : (?) *Mthiṅ-ril* : (?) **Skr. kādamba, a kind of goose with dark-grey wings.**

Dur-ba : (?) *Goose*

THE BACKGROUND OF THE BYA CHOS

THE *Bya chos* opens with a verse from the Buddhist Scriptures which reminds us that, in his infinite compassion, the Buddha has taught his doctrine not only to men, but to all living beings. It then goes on to tell us how the Dharma reached the birds, through the medium of a Bodhisattva disguised as a cuckoo. St. Francis also could not bear the thought that the birds might be beyond the pale of redemption, and so the most Buddhist of all Christian saints preached the doctrine of Jesus Christ to the birds who had gathered at his feet. Even the most tender-hearted Christian, however, is constrained to remain forever outside the world of the birds, while a Buddhist saint is endowed with facilities for penetrating directly into the various realms of life. He can become one of the birds, either by seeking rebirth among them, or by the method of magical transformation. In the *Jatakas* we read stories describing how the Lord Buddha, when still a Bodhisattva, was born as a peacock, a goose, a quail or a parrot. In this book it is the great Bodhisattva Avalokiteśvara who has 'transformed himself' (*sprul-nas*) into a cuckoo, and who initiates and guides the religious discussions of the assembled birds.

1. *Samantabhadracaryāpraṇidhānarāja* v. 19.

Why, we may ask, should just the cuckoo be the wisest, 'The Great Bird', 'The Great King of the Birds'? Is it perhaps the cavalier manner in which he disposes of his family responsibilities which endears him to Buddhist hearts? It is true that Buddhists in general are apt to regard family life as stuffy and depressing, to be forsaken for the freedom of a homeless existence. But the majority of Buddhists have never attributed to the cuckoo any exceptional wisdom. To the Japanese, for instance, he is, Professor Suzuki tells me, just a symbol of grief, its song being taken to convey the plaint of parted lovers. It is only in Lamaism that the cuckoo is so highly regarded, for reasons which are more ethnological than doctrinal. In Lamaist countries the Buddhists have been in contact and competition with the native Shamanism of the Bon religion. For the Bon[a], the cuckoo, 'the turquoise Bird', is the holy bird, the 'King of the Birds'. It is said to inspire the shamans. As one of them expresses it, "A small bird, with a blue breast, sits on a tree, hidden between a branch and the trunk, and there it shamanizes." With its song it gladdens the beings of the triple world, and the great teacher Gśen-rab taught the doctrine "with a lovely voice, like that of a Kokila," the Indian bird identified with the cuckoo. J. F. Rock[b] has published the picture of a Bon god of the Mo-so, who is flanked by two holy birds, the cuckoo and the Garuda (see p. 58). A generation ago, Maeterlinck maintained that "le grand secret des choses et du bonheur" could be symbolized by a

[a] H. Hoffmann, *Quellen zur Geschichte der tibetischen Bon Religion*, 1950, pp. 199–200.

[b] *Artibus Asiae*, VII, 1937.

'Blue Bird'. That may have been a distant echo of this tradition, although Maeterlinck slightly misrepresented it. A sentimentalist if ever there was one, he believed that the blue bird must be the turtle dove.

For 1,200 years Buddhist lamas have pursued the policy of rendering Bon beliefs innocuous by incorporating them into the framework of Buddhist orthodoxy. And this is what happened to the cuckoo when, inspired by an Indian story about prince Vikrama's change into a parrot[a], a lama of the Kahgyudpa sect composed in honour of Avalokiteśvara the popular story of 'Blue Neck' (*Nīlakantha*). The author was Mati, a monk of the *Gnubs* family, resident at the monastery of Drje-pong (*'bras-spuṅs*). The full title of his story is "The Tale (*avadāna*) of the Bird Blue-Neck, the Moon (of the doctrine), who has the Spirit of a Bodhisattva, – or Ear-rings for those who see through the unsubstantial Nature of this whole samsaric World".[b] The author claims that he just retells the story told to him by his master, the Lama Blo-bzaṅ Bstan-pa'i rgyal-mtshan of *Stag-phug*, who himself in a former life was its principal hero, – Dharmanandin, Prince of Benares.

It so happened that the prince fell deeply in love with one of his wives, neglecting all the others. In her jealousy, one of them, Svarasuti, complained to

[a]Much information on this can be found in M. Maurice Bloomfield, "On the art of entering another's body: a hindu fiction motif". *Proceedings of the American Philosophical Society*, vol. LVI, 1917, pp. 1–43.

[b]Byaṅ-chub sems-kyi sems mṅa-ba'i bya mgrin sṅon zla-ba 'i rtogs-pa brjod-pa, 'khor-ba 'i mtha' dag-la sñiṅ-po med-par mthoṅ-ba rnams-kyi rna rgyan. – Bacot's *Xylograph*, like that in the Library of the School of Oriental Studies, has 133 folios. The work was sufficiently popular to be translated into Mongol.

Lagaana, son of the prime minister, and the prince's closest friend, inciting him to seize the throne and to make her his queen. Persuaded by her, Lagaana planned to achieve their goal "by practising the transference into the body of the prince"..The narrator comments that when this decision had been reached "the Three Treasures knew that the prince would convert the world of the birds".

"To the north of the palace lay an ancient pleasure garden. Lagaana saw that the river Mahājana ran through it, and that in the hills, on the other bank of the river, lay a wood filled with wonders." He proposed to the prince that they should visit the park. The prince agreed and so "with a crowd of other young people they departed. The son of the minister then searched for the corpses of two cuckoos, fresh and without wounds, prayed to his personal god to grant him his desire, and stayed near the prince", who had sad forebodings, and prayed to the Three Treasures. "His heart was invaded by an infinite sadness. And a voice could be heard in the sky, saying:

'Quickly change your body, for the sake of creatures not human!

Do not re-enter the prince's body. Have courage!

A great work awaits you.

The people of Benares are to be pitied'."

So they went to the pleasure gardens, and on the opposite shore of the river they saw the wonderful forest. "As a result of his karma" the prince's heart was seduced by this sight, and he said: "We must certainly go and visit it. Run and fetch a boat from the palace!" Filled with joy, Lagaana gave him the corpses of the two cuckoos, without the other young men noticing it, and said to him: "Oh son of a god, let us perform the migration into these birds; then we shall be able to pass across."

The prinçe hesitated "because the migration is the secret teaching of the Brahmins, and is not meant for amusement", and also because he wanted first to ask his parents' permission. But Lagaana overcame his scruples and made him send away the pages. "The prince and Lagaana then entrusted their abandoned bodies to the protection of an Asura, entered into the fresh corpses of the two birds, and flew across to the other side of the river. While, enchanted with the spectacle, the prince enjoyed the fruits with a hundred savours and the shining flowers, the son of the prime minister, unseen by the prince, returned rapidly to the opposite bank. He entered the prince's body and threw his own into the river. Then he began to cry for help. To the pages who came running along, and who mistook him for the prince, he said, with tears in his eyes, that his dear friend, Lagaana, to amuse himself, had jumped into the river, and the river had carried him off. They all believed him, and said: 'Heavenly son, do not weep. As long as the prince is safe, what importance has even an able minister for the great people of Benares!'" So they spoke, and returned to Benares with him.

In the meantime the prince, because he had the nature of a cuckoo, flew here and there in search of fruits and flowers. After a while he wanted to rejoin his friend. For a long time he searched, but could not find him. He asked himself whether his friend had met with an accident, and, warned by a devaputra, he rushed back to the other bank. "He could not see either the bodies they had left there, nor the pages. Then he knew that his friend had undone the Transference, and had returned to the palace in Benares, while he himself was left, alone and helpless. The sun set. Overwhelmed by the horror of his situation, he now regretted that in the past he had not learned more about the holy doctrine."

"Night fell. No human voice, no dog barking. The birds, large and small, calling to each other, returned to their nests on the tops of the trees. Wild beasts howled, and prowled about. A cold wind blew up, and the prince shivered with despair and fright." He thought of his mother, and remembered her last words. After he had spent a terrible night on the top of a tree shaken by the storm, he was just about to fly to Benares, when the Bodhisattva Avalokiteśvara joined him in the form of a cuckoo, explained his friend's treason and ordered him to stay in order to convert the birds while he retained the shape of a bird.

The birds were at that time ruled by a parrot who could speak like a human being. With him the prince had many discussions about the holy doctrine, and gradually the feathered folk were won over to the Dharma.

As for Lagaana, when he returned to Benares, the prince's favourite wife doubted his identity, on account of his lack of devotion to the Buddhist faith. Lagaana drove her out and married Svarasuti. Many years later the prince, who had by then become a Bodhisattva, found his body again, and became king. Convinced of the irreality of the world, however, he soon abdicated and died in a deserted place.

This extremely popular story would be at the back of the minds of all Tibetans whenever the *Bya chos* is recited. The practice of soul-transference is one of the occult teachings of the Kahgyudpa school, and goes back to the Indian masters Tilopa and Naropa. Marpa (b. 993), 'the Translator', and the famous Milarepa (1038 – 1122), are among its Tibetan exponents. Some say that the secret has died with Marpa in 1081 A.D., while others assume[a] that it is still being practised. Alexandra David-Neel[b] gives a clear description of the practice. Although she is generally a believer, she adds that the stories told about it "may well be regarded as fable" and the story of Blue-Neck says that "generally speaking this practice is prohibited and of little use".[c]

The Tibetan term *'pho-ba groṅ-'jug* is the translation of the sanskrit *para-śarīra-āveśa*, or *para-kāya-praveśa*, which means literally "entering into another's body". From the point of view of orthodox Buddhism the practice represents an intrusion of popular beliefs. If the exit of the soul from the body is compared with "a bird flying out of an open skylight", this animistic presupposition is not easy to reconcile with the Buddhists *anattā* doctrine. Marpa performed the miracle in a state of trance, with the help of mantras he had learned in India. To judge from his biography[d], he used this performance to demonstrate his spiritual prowess to astonished witnesses, with the aim of converting them to the

[a]Evans-Wentz, *Tibetan Yoga and Secret Doctrines*, 1935, pp. 254 and 257. For some details see pp. 169–70, and 246–76.

[b]*With Mystics and Magicians in Tibet*, 1936, pp. 275–78.

[c]spyir tshul 'di lta-bu dgag bya che shiṅ dgos-pa chuṅ na'aṅ.

[d]J. Bacot, *La vie de Marpa, le 'Traducteur'*, Paris 1937.

religious life. In one instance a young pigeon, chased by a hawk, died from fright. Marpa abandoned his body, leaving it on the ground looking like a corpse, and reanimated the pigeon, which flew up to rejoin its mother. A friend begged him to come back, the pigeon fell down, Marpa got up, laughed, and said:

"*This body I abandoned, like an empty house;*
Into a pigeon's body I transferred myself.
Spreading their wings, and flying up, in love,
The mother and her little one have found each other.
All those who saw it wondered greatly."

The method apparently also had a deeper meaning in that it made it possible to "gain Nirvana without meditating", but the biography does not make the connection very clear.[a] It could further be used to choose a rebirth at will, by reanimating the fresh corpse of an animal or human being at the moment of death.

Looking back we can now distinguish a fivefold tradition behind the *Bya chos:* 1. The universal Buddhist belief that the Dharma of the Buddha is not confined to men, but addressed to all beings, including animals and ghosts. 2. The Mahayana belief that the great Bodhisattva of mercy, Avalokiteśvara, the Kwan-yin of the Chinese, takes on many forms in his urge to help living beings and to turn their minds towards Nirvana. The majority of the audience would take it for granted that Avalokiteśvara, whom they

[a]The connection may lie in the "transference into the Dharmabody" during the first stage of the Bardo, about which we can read in Evans-Wentz on page 247.

know as Chenrezi, resides among them in the shape of the Dalai Lama. There was thus nothing surprising about the idea that among birds he should live as a bird. 3. The belief, derived from the Bon religion and confined to Lamaism, that the cuckoo is a holy bird. 4. The well-known Tibetan novel which connects 'Blue-Neck' with soul-transference, a miraculous practice which has always greatly fascinated the inhabitants of Tibet. 5. A great number of bird-dialogues as well known in the folk-poetry of Tibet as in that of China. Here that literary form has been adopted to serve Buddhist teachings. We must always bear in mind that the poems are meant to be sung. Refrains like *kiki*, which slightly disturb the rhythm when read, round off each line very effectively in song.

We could add that religious mystics have at all times felt a strong affinity with the birds, whose life seemed to exemplify the freedom they longed for. The saints have their range in the Void, and one can no more discern their tracks than those of the birds through the sky. So a famous verse of the *Dhammapada* (v. 93). It is among the Persian Sufis that we find the closest parallel to the *Bya chos*. In Farid ud-Din Attar's "Conference of the Birds", the birds gather under the leadership of the Phoenix, and after much conversation they set out on their journey back to the divine fountain of all life. And so greatly were the Buddhist contemplatives enamoured of birds, that they could not conceive the Paradise of Amitabha, situated on a distant star in the West, to exist without them. For reasons of dogma that Paradise, as a 'Pure Land', could harbour no animals.[a] But,

[a]See No. 177 in "Buddhist Texts through the Ages", ed. E. Conze, 1954.

since without bird-songs the happiness of its inhabitants would be incomplete, the Tathagata, by his magic, "conjures up" (*nirmita*) "flocks of immortal (*amara*) birds", who "three times every night, and three times every day, come together and perform a concert, each uttering his own note" and all proclaiming the praise of the Buddha and of the religious virtues. "When the men in that Paradise hear their songs, their minds are turned to the Buddha, to the Dharma, and to the Samgha."[a] By contrast we hear of an ascetic named Udraka, who was disturbed in his meditations by the singing of birds, and wished that they were all dead. He had to suffer in hell for a long time as a consequence of this wish.[b]

It has not always been easy to identify the birds which take part in this congress. Some are not given at all in the dictionaries, others wrongly. For the ornithological details I must refer the reader to the handbooks of the naturalists.[c] The parrot, "skilled in speech", is of course the green Parakeet. The *'jol-mo*, whom I have called a 'thrush', is a singing bird found in the Juniper groves near Lhasa. Its voice is greatly admired; what is meant here is probably a species of the Chinese oriole. The 'eagle' (p. 15) may not be an 'eagle' at all. The Tibetan word *khyuṅ* really means the mythical bird Garūda. And Salim Ali[d] tells us that he has found "in different parts of India the

[a] Sukhāvatīvyūha. Large text, par. 40. Short text, par. 6.

[b] Nagarjuna, *Le traité de la grande vertue de sagesse*, trad. E. Lamotte II, 1949, p. 1050 sq.

[c] Salim Ali: *The Book of Indian Birds*, 4th ed., 1946, Bombay. *Indian Hill Birds*, OUP, 1949. H. Whistler, *Popular Handbook of Indian Birds*, 1949.

[d] *Indian Birds*, p. IV.

name Garūda applied to the Vulture as well as to the Hornbill and the Green Pigeon, the general tendency" being "to call any large bird Garūda". I have followed the French in translating *lto-dur* by 'kite' (p. 46), although I see in Bell that the kite is called piṅ kyu-ma. No great zoological precision can, in any case, be expected from a peasant literature.

Almost all the birds repeat at the end of each verse some stereotyped saying which I have given in Tibetan, followed by the translation. In the case of the Cuckoo and the Kestrel this keynote imitates the cry of the bird, i.e. *kukhu* and *kiki*. In other cases the call of the birds bears no resemblance to the sounds attributed to them here. Nothing could, for instance be more unlike the hoopoe's (*pu-śud*) *hoo-po hoo-po-po* than the *mi 'ju kha tsha* it utters here, and even the peacock's *may-awé* is only imperfectly reproduced by his *kog-go* in the *Bya chos*. Sometimes the bird's utterance is clearly a reflection of its Tibetan name. The cock's *e-go* rhymes with *depho*, his name; the jackdaw, *skyuṅ-ka*, does not here say *tshak*, as in the Natural History books, but *khu-skyuṅ*, and similarly the wagtail, *tiṅ-tiṅ-ma*, repeats *gtiṅ riṅ*, instead of the *chi-chip* which ordinary mortals hear. Other refrains, again, remain quite mysterious and inexplicable. We may perhaps assume that our Lama was a saintly man, gifted with the supernatural power of understanding the speech of birds (*ruta-jñāna*), which is the reward of prolonged austerities and solitary meditations. This gift would also have given him a clue to some of the strange words in this book, such as *ema*, which are not noted in the dictionaries, and which I have interpreted as best I could. If I had, like Siegfried, dipped my limbs into the dragon's blood, I would be more confident about my knowledge of the speech of birds than I am now.

It is debatable how far the speeches are characteristic of the individual birds to which they are attributed. Each civilization has its own conception of the personalities of its birds, depending on numerous associations which go back to folk-lore, religion and literature (from which we know, for instance, that the owl is the bird of Minerva). In England one speaks proverbially of someone being 'as happy as a lark', but in Tibet (p. 29) the lark seems to be regarded as a pretty lugubrious bird. At present we do not know enough to work out these associations for Tibet. But when, for instance, the peacock is mentioned, a Tibetan listener would not only think of the appearance of the bird, but also remember its symbolic meaning within the doctrine of Buddhism. Mahāmayūrī, the Great Peahen, is one of the deities of northern Buddhism. Even those who have never read the Tantric scriptures, would still be familiar with her sacred aspect through the ritual dances which are performed in monasteries on certain festival days, or through the ceremonial dances (*bro khrag-po*) of small troupes of wandering dancers so well known to everybody. One such troupe, belonging to the Kahgyudpa sect, and described by H. Siiger[a], impersonated peacocks in several of their dances; in one of them the bird "makes three graceful salutations" (*Phyag-'bul legs gsum bar śig*), just as in our poem.

The illustrations on the cover are taken from a Tibetan work on pharmacology in the Royal Library

[a]"Dancing Pilgrims from Tibet." *Geografisk Tideskrift*, 1951, 26 pp.

of Copenhagen[a], which in this part goes back to a well-known Chinese treatise of the Ming period, the *Pên ts'ao*. Each drawing is accompanied by the name in Tibetan, Chinese and Manchu. Out of the 26 birds in our book, 15 appear in the illustrations. Their names are given in italics in the following list:

Folio 22 (*s. back of jacket, first strip, from left to right*):

1. Phoenix
2. *Peacock*
3. *Hazel Grouse*
4. *Partridge*
5. *Jackdaw*
6. *Crow*
7. Pheasant
8. *Thrush*
9. *Parrot*
10. Bustard
11. *Pigeon*
12. *Cuckoo*
13. Magpie
14. *Myna*

Folio 23 (*s. second strip*):

1. *Hoopoe*
2. Whiteheaded Laughing Thrush
3. Woodpecker
4. Swallow
5. ?

[a]Dri med śel-phreṅ-nas bśad-pa 'i sman-gyi 'khruṅs-dpe mdzes mtshar mig rgyan. The author is 'Tsho byed-kyi rig-pa smra-ba'i dge-sloṅ Ye-śes don-grub bstan-pa'i rgyal-mtshan. – 34 folios. The birds are found on folios 22–26, of which we have reproduced folios 22–4.

6. Weaver Bird
7. *Lark*
8. Quail

Folio 24 (*s. third strip*):
1. *Owl*
2. Sparrow Hawk
3. *Owlet*
4. Hobby
5. Small Hobby
6. Drongoe

The illustrations on pp. 48 and 62 come from the same work. The other illustrations are taken from the Ming encyclopedia, *San ts'ai t'u hui.*

Vulture

Notes

1 (p. 15). The present aeon is called 'auspicious' (*bhadrakalpa*), because in the course of it more Buddhas are said to make their appearance than in most aeons, – a thousand of them, to be more accurate, as against the usual three or four.

2 (p. 15). The original Saraha was a Buddhist sage and magician who lived in India in the 6th century. Many masters of the Kahgyudpa school have adopted this name, which, as H. Meyer points out, 'designated here the type of the perfect man, who is both a saint and a worker of miracles'.

3 (p. 17). Avalokita is the Lord who 'looks down from on high'. The sanskrit equivalent for 'surveyed', *avalokya*, is a play on his name.

4 (p. 21). *Byas-pas rtsa-ba dam chos 'di go dgos*. I have not been able to make sense of this line as it stands. I suspect that the text may be faulty. Or perhaps *grol-ba'i* should be understood after *byas-pas*.

5 (p. 22). *'jur-gegs*. A kind of *Yi-dag* whose throat is so contracted that a drop of water can hardly pass through it to quench his ever-burning thirst. (Das, *Tibetan Dictionary*.)

6 (p. 23). These 'fairies' are called *mkha'-gro*, literally 'sky-walkers'. Their mode of life is such that they deserve a name framed in analogy to the more familiar 'street-walkers'.

7 (p. 23). i.e. from Maitreya, the coming Buddha, who dwells at present in the Tushita heavens. The help he can give is twofold: one may either visit him in trance to receive inspiration about the doctrine, as Asaṅga and others did in days past. This inspiration is gained by an 'unwavering and supramundane' trance which resembles 'the radiant light of the sun', and leads to an 'outpouring of the Dharma'. Or, after death, one may be reborn in his presence, and mystical contemplation is one of the most important means for gaining rebirth in the Tushita heavens.

8 (p. 25). 'Iron age', – this is rather free for *bskal-pa sñigs-ma*, more literally, 'degenerate age'. The sanskrit equivalent is *kashāya*, and denotes the present Kaliyuga, in which everything decays and degenerates.

9 (p. 26). Because one will be reborn as a Preta. (See note 14.)

10 (p. 30). *Chos med skor zan-gyi lus sgyur 'di ci byed.* The sentence is rather obscure. *Chos med skor* is an 'irreligious environment'. The difficulty lies in the word *sgyur*, which means 'transformation' according to Das, but it is not clear to me what kind of 'transformation' is intended here.

11 (p. 30). i.e. a Yogin cannot achieve full certainty as long as his practices and meditations fall short of perfection.

12 (p. 30). The 'dharma which transcends the whole of Samsara' is Nirvana. The allusion is here to one of the more obscure teachings of Buddhism. Nirvana is said to be 'signless', in other words, it has no marks at all, and it cannot therefore be recognized as such. This excludes certainty, as it is usually understood. The reader who finds this hard to grasp is well advised to pass on.

13 (p. 31). The translation here omits two verses which are hopelessly obscure: *skya rgyal-gyi rkub-la tig tig med/grod 'gran-gi dman-la tig tig med.* The second verse means: 'In the base pleasures of the belly, – no certainty.' H. Meyer translates the first tentatively as: 'Au revers des amulettes: pas de certitude.' *rkub-pa* is 'backside', but also 'anus' and 'vulva'. Perhaps a sexual reference? I have asked a number of travellers to Tibet, and it does honour to their moral character that none of them could shed any light on it. 'In the slip of the victorious thrust, – no certainty' might perhaps not be too far out.

14 (p. 33). The Pretas are ghosts who have enormous bellies and very tiny mouths. Barely any food and drink manages to get through the mouth, and their distended bellies are therefore as hot as furnaces from hunger and thirst.

15 (p. 35). The existence of the ovum remaining unsuspected until the invention of the microscope, the Tibetans assumed that blood is the woman's contribution to the embryo.

16 (p. 37). At the very centre of our minds is an absolute thought, which is the basic reality in our being, and which we can reach by introspective meditation. The cuckoo here expounds the metaphysics of the Yogacarins. See E. Conze, *Buddhism*, 1953, pp. 166–71.

17 (p. 40). *sñiṅ-rje byaṅ-sems ldan-pa khyod.* Literally: "You who are endowed with compassion and the thought of enlightenment." This is a way of saying that the cuckoo is a Bodhisattva, for the characteristic of a Bodhisattva is that, from compassion for all beings, he makes a vow to gain enlightenment for the benefit of others and to help others to win enlightenment in their turn.

18 (p. 41). *chos brgyad* = *'jig-rten-kyi chos brgyad* = the eight laukika dharmas, which are: gain and loss, respect and contempt, good luck and bad luck, praise and blame.

19 (p. 42). Literally: "Do not take it up, for it will burn your mouth." The first two syllables are, probably deliberately, ambiguous, and may also mean 'indigestible'.

20 (p. 43). *skya min ser min-gyi gšin-po'i lto-skal mi 'ju kha tsha.* Literally: "Of those who are neither whitish nor yellow, the portion of the food reserved for the deceased, – do not take it up, etc." This is rather puzzling. *Ser-skya* can also mean, 'tawny, brown'. H. Meyer has the following note: "It is usual in Tibet to arrange funeral repasts. A portion of the food, destined for the deceased, is burnt in order to appease his hunger and thirst. It is a great sin not to perform this rite. 'Those who are neither grey nor yellow' are surely those who have failed in their duties towards the dead." There is some probability in this, but further research is required.

21 (p. 43). Aggregate, *phuṅ-po*, literally 'skandha'. Different persons are regarded as as many 'heaps' of five aggregates, i.e. of form, feelings, perceptions, impulses, and acts of consciousness.

22 (p. 45). Stupas are often white with the droppings of pigeons, and the pigeon here promises to be more careful in future.

23 (p. 45). The point of this promise seems to lie in the fact that the nest of the hoopoe, always in some dark place, "becomes very offensive and smelly," because it is never cleaned out. (Hugh Whistler, *Popular Handbook of Indian Birds*, 1935, p. 272.)